PRINCEWILL LAGANG

Edu-preneurs: Revolutionizing Education through Entrepreneurship

First published by PRINCEWILL LAGANG 2023

Copyright © 2023 by Princewill Lagang

All rights reserved. No part of this publication may be reproduced, stored or transmitted in any form or by any means, electronic, mechanical, photocopying, recording, scanning, or otherwise without written permission from the publisher. It is illegal to copy this book, post it to a website, or distribute it by any other means without permission.

Princewill Lagang asserts the moral right to be identified as the author of this work.

First edition

This book was professionally typeset on Reedsy. Find out more at reedsy.com

Contents

1. Edu-preneurs: Revolutionizing Education through...   1
2. The Birth of Edu-preneurship   4
3. Edu-preneurial Mindset and Skillset   7
4. Edu-preneurial Models of Education   11
5. Innovations in EdTech: Transforming Learning Through...   14
6. Alternative Schools and Innovative Learning Environments   18
7. Social Enterprises: Educating with Purpose   22
8. Open Educational Resources (OER): Democratizing Learning   25
9. Teacher-Led Innovations: Transforming Education from Within   29
10. Edu-preneurship in Policy and Advocacy: Shaping the Future...   32
11. The Global Perspective: Edu-preneurship and International...   35
12. Edu-preneurship: Challenges, Ethical Considerations, and the...   38
13. Summary   41

1

Edu-preneurs: Revolutionizing Education through Entrepreneurship

In a small, unassuming classroom on the outskirts of a bustling metropolis, a group of young students gathers around a table covered in papers, notebooks, and colorful markers. This is not your typical classroom, and these are not your typical students. This is the dawn of a new era in education, a movement fueled by innovation, creativity, and a profound sense of purpose. This is the world of "Edu-preneurs."

Introduction: The Changing Landscape of Education

The 21st century has witnessed an unprecedented transformation in education. Traditional models of teaching and learning have been challenged by an ever-evolving global landscape, rapid technological advancements, and a growing demand for personalized, relevant, and engaging educational experiences. It's a world where the classroom is no longer confined to four walls, where teachers are not just purveyors of knowledge but facilitators of discovery, and where students are not passive recipients but active architects of their learning journeys.

As our world has changed, so too must our approach to education. We find ourselves in an age where entrepreneurial thinking and innovation have become indispensable tools for reshaping education for the better. Edu-preneurs, a new breed of educators and innovators, are leading the charge in this education revolution.

Defining Edu-preneurs

But who are these Edu-preneurs, and what sets them apart? Edu-preneurs are individuals who have a passion for education, a keen sense of entrepreneurship, and a relentless drive to effect meaningful change in the way we learn and teach. They are visionaries who challenge the status quo, disrupt traditional educational paradigms, and inspire a new generation of students to become lifelong learners and creative problem-solvers.

Edu-preneurs come from diverse backgrounds and professions. They may be teachers, parents, students, or professionals from various industries. What unites them is their unwavering commitment to improving education and their willingness to take risks, experiment with novel approaches, and collaborate across disciplines to achieve their goals.

The Need for Edu-preneurs

Why do we need Edu-preneurs in education? The answer lies in the many challenges that the education system faces today:

1. Technological Transformation: The digital age has brought forth a myriad of technological tools and platforms that can enhance the learning experience. Edu-preneurs harness these technologies to create dynamic, interactive, and personalized educational content.

2. Diverse Learning Needs: Students are not uniform in their learning styles and abilities. Edu-preneurs understand that one size does not fit all and work

to tailor education to individual needs and preferences.

3. Globalization: As our world becomes more interconnected, there is a growing demand for students to have a global perspective. Edu-preneurs develop programs that expose students to diverse cultures and perspectives.

4. Lifelong Learning: In the age of rapidly changing job markets, lifelong learning is essential. Edu-preneurs create platforms and opportunities for continuous skill development.

5. Engagement and Motivation: Traditional education often falls short in engaging and motivating students. Edu-preneurs use gamification, storytelling, and other innovative techniques to make learning exciting and inspiring.

The Structure of This Book

In this book, we will explore the world of Edu-preneurs and how they are revolutionizing education through entrepreneurship. Each chapter will delve into a different aspect of this transformative movement, from the stories of inspiring Edu-preneurs to the practical strategies and tools they employ. We will examine case studies, interview leading Edu-preneurs, and offer insights into how you can become an Edu-preneur or support their work.

As we embark on this journey, it is our hope that you will gain a deeper understanding of the immense potential of Edu-preneurs to shape the future of education. Whether you are a student, educator, parent, policymaker, or anyone passionate about learning, this book is your guide to the exciting world of Edu-preneurs and their mission to revolutionize education for the better. So, let's dive in and discover how Edu-preneurs are leading the charge in this educational transformation, one innovative idea at a time.

2

The Birth of Edu-preneurship

In the previous chapter, we explored the concept of Edu-preneurs and why their role is critical in reshaping the landscape of education. In this chapter, we will take a closer look at the origins of Edu-preneurship, the driving forces that led to its emergence, and the early pioneers who paved the way for this transformative movement.

A Historical Perspective

Edu-preneurship did not emerge overnight but rather evolved over time in response to changing societal needs and the relentless pursuit of better educational outcomes. The roots of Edu-preneurship can be traced back to several historical and philosophical underpinnings:

1. Progressive Education Movements: Early pioneers such as John Dewey and Maria Montessori challenged traditional teaching methods and advocated for more student-centered, experiential, and hands-on learning approaches. These ideas laid the groundwork for Edu-preneurship.

2. The Digital Revolution: The advent of the personal computer and the

internet in the late 20th century opened up new possibilities for educational innovation. E-learning, online courses, and digital resources began to reshape the way we access and acquire knowledge.

3. Globalization: The globalization of information and knowledge exchange created an awareness of the need for cross-cultural and global perspectives in education. Edu-preneurs saw opportunities to bridge cultural gaps and promote international collaboration in learning.

4. Economic Realities: The ever-changing job market and the need for continuous skill development led to a recognition that traditional education was not preparing individuals adequately for the future. Edu-preneurs sought to address this gap.

Early Edu-preneurs: Pioneering the Movement

As Edu-preneurship started to take shape, a few visionaries emerged as early champions of this movement. They were the trailblazers who dared to think differently about education and took bold steps to implement their innovative ideas:

1. Sugata Mitra: Mitra is known for his "Hole in the Wall" experiment, which demonstrated that children can teach themselves using computers and the internet. His work laid the foundation for self-directed and technology-enhanced learning.

2. Sal Khan: Founder of Khan Academy, Khan created a free, online platform offering educational videos in various subjects. His initiative made high-quality education accessible to anyone with an internet connection and demonstrated the power of online learning.

3. Gever Tulley: Tulley founded the Tinkering School, a program that allows children to engage in hands-on, experiential learning by building and creating.

His approach exemplified the idea of learning by doing, a key concept in Edu-preneurship.

The Edu-preneurial Ecosystem

The rise of Edu-preneurship was not solely due to the efforts of a few individuals. It required the development of a supportive ecosystem, including incubators, educational technology companies, funding sources, and collaborations with schools and educational institutions. This ecosystem encouraged and nurtured the growth of Edu-preneurship by providing the infrastructure and resources necessary for innovation to thrive.

Current Trends and Challenges

As we move further into the 21st century, Edu-preneurship continues to evolve and face new challenges. The landscape is dynamic, with trends such as the use of artificial intelligence in education, the rise of adaptive learning platforms, and the push for open educational resources. At the same time, Edu-preneurs must address issues related to data privacy, equity, and the impact of technology on social and emotional development.

In this chapter, we've traced the historical roots of Edu-preneurship, examined the early pioneers who laid the groundwork, and discussed the development of the Edu-preneurial ecosystem. As we move forward in this book, we'll explore how these early ideas and innovations have blossomed into a dynamic, ever-evolving movement that is transforming education around the world.

3

Edu-preneurial Mindset and Skillset

In the previous chapters, we discussed the emergence of Edu-preneurship and its historical roots. Now, we dive deeper into the core elements that define an Edu-preneur: the mindset and skillset that enable them to drive innovation and change in education.

The Edu-preneurial Mindset

Edu-preneurs possess a distinct mindset that sets them apart from traditional educators. This mindset is characterized by several key attributes:

1. Innovation and Creativity: Edu-preneurs are natural innovators. They constantly seek new and creative ways to improve education, whether it's through the use of technology, teaching methods, or curriculum design.

2. Adaptability: The education landscape is ever-evolving. Edu-preneurs are adaptable and open to change, willing to pivot when needed to better meet the needs of students and the demands of the future.

3. Risk-Taking: Edu-preneurs are not afraid to take calculated risks. They

understand that trying new things and pushing boundaries are essential to driving meaningful change in education.

4. Empathy: They have a deep understanding of the needs and emotions of students, parents, and educators. Empathy allows Edu-preneurs to design solutions that truly resonate with the educational community.

5. Resilience: Edu-preneurs encounter challenges and setbacks but maintain a strong sense of purpose. Their resilience enables them to persevere in the face of adversity.

6. Global Perspective: They see the importance of preparing students for a globalized world. Edu-preneurs appreciate the value of cross-cultural understanding and international collaboration.

7. Social Impact: Beyond profit, Edu-preneurs are motivated by the desire to create positive social impact. They seek to improve access to quality education and address educational inequities.

Developing the Edu-preneurial Mindset

While some individuals may naturally exhibit these qualities, the Edu-preneurial mindset can also be cultivated and nurtured. Here are strategies for developing an Edu-preneurial mindset:

1. Continuous Learning: Stay curious and committed to lifelong learning. Explore new subjects, learn from diverse perspectives, and embrace challenges as opportunities for growth.

2. Networking: Connect with like-minded individuals, attend conferences, and engage in discussions on education and entrepreneurship. Building a strong network can provide support and inspiration.

3. Mentorship: Seek out mentors who have experience in both education and entrepreneurship. Their guidance and advice can be invaluable in shaping your mindset.

4. Practice Empathy: Develop a deep understanding of the needs and emotions of those you aim to serve in the education sector. Listen actively and empathize with their challenges and aspirations.

5. Learn from Failure: Embrace failure as a learning opportunity. Every setback can teach you something valuable and lead to greater success in the future.

The Edu-preneurial Skillset

In addition to the mindset, Edu-preneurs possess a unique skillset that equips them to drive innovation and create change in education:

1. Technology Proficiency: Edu-preneurs are comfortable with educational technology and can leverage it to enhance the learning experience.

2. Data Analysis: They can collect and analyze data to inform decision-making, track student progress, and measure the impact of their initiatives.

3. Curriculum Design: Edu-preneurs understand how to design and adapt curricula to suit the needs of students in a dynamic world.

4. Project Management: They can efficiently manage and execute complex educational projects, coordinating the efforts of teams and partners.

5. Funding and Resource Acquisition: Edu-preneurs have the ability to secure funding, whether through grants, investors, or other sources, to support their initiatives.

6. Communication and Advocacy: They can effectively communicate their vision and advocate for change, both within the education community and with stakeholders and policymakers.

The Journey of Becoming an Edu-preneur

The development of an Edu-preneurial mindset and skillset is an ongoing journey. Edu-preneurs continually refine these attributes as they gain experience and confront the challenges and opportunities that arise in the field of education. In the chapters to come, we will explore how Edu-preneurs apply these qualities to create innovative solutions and drive meaningful change in education.

4

Edu-preneurial Models of Education

In the previous chapters, we've discussed the emergence of Edu-preneurship, the mindset and skillset of Edu-preneurs, and the historical roots of this transformative movement. Now, we delve into the various models and approaches Edu-preneurs employ to revolutionize education. These models are as diverse as the Edu-preneurs themselves, reflecting the innovative, dynamic nature of this field.

Edu-preneurial Models: A Spectrum of Innovation

Edu-preneurship encompasses a wide spectrum of approaches, from small-scale, grassroots initiatives to large-scale, systemic changes. Edu-preneurs operate within various contexts, each with its unique set of challenges and opportunities. Here are some Edu-preneurial models that span this spectrum:

1. EdTech Startups: Edu-preneurs often create educational technology (EdTech) startups that develop apps, platforms, and software designed to enhance the learning experience. These technologies can range from personalized learning tools to virtual reality simulations.

2. Alternative Schools and Learning Centers: Some Edu-preneurs establish alternative schools and learning centers that provide unique, experiential, or project-based learning opportunities. These models focus on student engagement and hands-on experiences.

3. Social Enterprises: Edu-preneurs in social enterprises combine profit-making with a mission to address educational inequities. They often provide affordable or free education to underserved communities, relying on innovative business models to sustain their efforts.

4. Open Educational Resources (OER): Edu-preneurs in this model develop and share educational content, such as textbooks, videos, and course materials, freely accessible to learners worldwide. They aim to democratize education by reducing costs and increasing access.

5. Teacher-Led Innovations: Some Edu-preneurs are educators who pioneer new teaching methods, curricula, or school programs within traditional educational institutions. They work to innovate from within the system.

6. Global Collaborations and Exchange Programs: Edu-preneurs create platforms and programs that connect students from different countries, fostering cross-cultural understanding and international collaboration.

7. Education Policy and Advocacy: While not traditional Edu-preneurs, individuals working in policy and advocacy play a crucial role in driving systemic change in education. They advocate for reforms that align with Edu-preneurial principles.

Case Studies in Edu-preneurial Models

Let's explore a few Edu-preneurial models through real-world case studies:

1. EdTech Startup: Khan Academy

Sal Khan's Khan Academy, a non-profit organization, offers free, world-class education to anyone, anywhere. Their platform provides instructional videos, practice exercises, and a personalized learning dashboard. It's a prime example of how technology can revolutionize learning.

2. Alternative School: High Tech High

High Tech High, located in San Diego, California, is an innovative K-12 school system that emphasizes project-based learning and real-world experiences. Its Edu-preneurial approach focuses on student engagement and skills development.

3. Social Enterprise: Bridge International Academies

Bridge International Academies operates a network of affordable, high-quality schools across Africa and Asia. Their model uses technology and standardized curricula to provide education in underserved communities.

4. OER: MIT OpenCourseWare

The Massachusetts Institute of Technology (MIT) offers free access to nearly all of its course content through MIT OpenCourseWare. This initiative demonstrates how open educational resources can extend the reach of prestigious institutions to a global audience.

Key Takeaways

In this chapter, we explored the diverse Edu-preneurial models of education, from EdTech startups to alternative schools, social enterprises, and open educational resources. Edu-preneurs employ these models to tackle the challenges and opportunities within the education landscape, pushing the boundaries of traditional education and advocating for change. In the chapters ahead, we will delve deeper into each of these models, examining their impact, success stories, and the challenges Edu-preneurs face in implementing them.

5

Innovations in EdTech: Transforming Learning Through Technology

In this chapter, we'll delve into one of the most prominent and transformative aspects of Edu-preneurship: innovations in Educational Technology (EdTech). The integration of technology in education has become a driving force behind many Edu-preneurial endeavors, reshaping how students learn and educators teach.

The EdTech Revolution

The 21st century has seen a remarkable integration of technology in education, revolutionizing the way knowledge is accessed and delivered. From interactive online platforms to AI-driven personalized learning, EdTech is rapidly transforming the educational landscape. Edu-preneurs have been at the forefront of this revolution, designing, developing, and implementing cutting-edge technologies that enhance the learning experience.

Key EdTech Innovations

1. Online Learning Platforms: The advent of online learning platforms like

Coursera, edX, and Udemy has made high-quality education accessible to learners around the world. These platforms offer courses on a wide range of subjects, allowing students to study at their own pace and schedule.

2. Adaptive Learning Systems: Adaptive learning platforms use algorithms and data analytics to personalize the learning experience for each student. These systems adjust the difficulty and content of lessons based on a student's progress and performance, ensuring that they receive instruction tailored to their needs.

3. Virtual Reality (VR) and Augmented Reality (AR): VR and AR technologies are being used to create immersive educational experiences. Students can explore historical sites, dissect virtual specimens, or engage in interactive simulations, bringing learning to life.

4. Gamification: Gamification techniques are employed to make learning more engaging and fun. By incorporating game elements such as rewards, challenges, and leaderboards, EdTech platforms motivate students to stay motivated and progress.

5. Artificial Intelligence (AI): AI-powered educational tools offer intelligent content recommendations, automated grading, and even virtual teaching assistants. These technologies can provide personalized feedback and insights to both students and educators.

6. Blended Learning: Blended learning combines traditional classroom instruction with online resources and platforms. Edu-preneurs have been instrumental in designing and implementing these blended learning models.

EdTech Success Stories

Let's take a look at a few EdTech success stories to illustrate the impact of Edu-preneurs in this field:

1. Duolingo: Luis von Ahn and Severin Hacker co-founded Duolingo, a language learning platform that has made learning a new language accessible and engaging for millions of users worldwide.

2. Kahoot!: Johan Brand and Jamie Brooker launched Kahoot!, a game-based learning platform that allows educators to create interactive quizzes and games for their students. It's become a staple in many classrooms, increasing student engagement and participation.

3. Coursera: Daphne Koller and Andrew Ng co-founded Coursera, a massive open online course (MOOC) platform that partners with universities and organizations to offer online courses. Coursera has brought high-quality education to a global audience.

Challenges in EdTech

Despite the tremendous potential of EdTech, there are also challenges that Edu-preneurs face in this space:

1. Equity and Access: Ensuring that technology-driven education is accessible to all students, including those in underserved communities, is a critical challenge.

2. Data Privacy: The collection and use of student data raise concerns about privacy and security. Edu-preneurs must navigate these issues while providing personalized learning experiences.

3. Teacher Training: Integrating technology effectively into the classroom requires ongoing teacher training and support, which can be a logistical and financial challenge.

4. Digital Divide: Not all students have access to the necessary devices and internet connectivity. Bridging the digital divide is essential to making

EdTech truly inclusive.

The Future of EdTech and Edu-preneurship

EdTech continues to evolve at a rapid pace, and Edu-preneurs are poised to play a significant role in shaping the future of education. The integration of emerging technologies like AI, VR, and blockchain in education, along with the global expansion of online learning, promises an exciting and dynamic landscape for Edu-preneurship in the years to come.

In the next chapter, we'll explore another Edu-preneurial model—alternative schools and innovative learning environments—and how they are redefining traditional educational settings.

6

Alternative Schools and Innovative Learning Environments

In this chapter, we'll explore the Edu-preneurial model of alternative schools and innovative learning environments. These models challenge traditional educational settings and offer creative approaches to teaching and learning.

The Need for Alternative Education

Traditional educational systems, while effective for many, may not meet the diverse needs of all students. There is a growing recognition that one-size-fits-all education can leave some learners disengaged or underserved. Alternative schools and innovative learning environments aim to address these gaps by providing unique, student-centered approaches to education.

Key Characteristics of Alternative Schools and Innovative Learning Environments

1. Student-Centered Learning: These settings prioritize the needs and

interests of individual students. The curriculum is often personalized, and students have a say in their own learning experiences.

2. Experiential Learning: Alternative schools emphasize hands-on, experiential learning. Students engage in real-world projects, field trips, and activities that connect classroom learning to practical applications.

3. Project-Based Learning: Project-based learning is a common pedagogical approach in these environments. Students work on projects, often collaboratively, to develop critical thinking, problem-solving, and teamwork skills.

4. Flexibility: Alternative schools may have flexible schedules, allowing students to learn at their own pace. Some offer options for remote or online learning to accommodate individual needs.

5. Small Class Sizes: Smaller class sizes enable more personalized instruction and one-on-one interactions between students and teachers.

6. Emphasis on Creativity and Arts: Many alternative schools place a strong emphasis on the arts, creativity, and self-expression, recognizing their importance in holistic development.

7. Diverse Assessment Methods: Alternative schools often use diverse assessment methods beyond traditional testing, such as portfolios, presentations, and peer evaluations.

Success Stories in Alternative Education

Several alternative schools and innovative learning environments have gained recognition for their unique approaches and impact on students. Here are a few success stories:

1. Sudbury Valley School: Founded in 1968, Sudbury Valley School in

Massachusetts operates on the principles of self-directed learning and student democracy. Students have the freedom to choose what they study and how they spend their time.

2. Big Picture Learning: This network of schools around the world embraces internships, real-world experiences, and personalized learning plans. Students are encouraged to explore their passions and interests.

3. High Tech High: Based in San Diego, High Tech High is a network of charter schools known for its project-based learning approach. Students collaborate on projects that address real-world problems.

Challenges and Criticisms

While alternative schools and innovative learning environments offer numerous advantages, they are not without challenges and criticisms:

1. Accountability: Critics argue that the lack of standardized testing and traditional assessments makes it challenging to evaluate the effectiveness of alternative education models.

2. Equity: Ensuring that alternative schools are accessible to all students, including those from underserved communities, is a significant challenge. Funding and resources may be limited.

3. Transition to College or Career: Some question whether students from alternative schools are adequately prepared for the transition to higher education or the workforce, given the non-traditional nature of their education.

4. Teacher Training: Educators in alternative schools may require different training and support to effectively implement student-centered and project-based approaches.

The Future of Alternative Education and Edu-preneurship

The future of alternative schools and innovative learning environments is promising. Edu-preneurs are continually experimenting with new models and approaches to education, addressing the diverse needs of students and creating more inclusive, engaging, and effective learning environments. As we move forward in this book, we'll explore other Edu-preneurial models and their contributions to the transformation of education.

7

Social Enterprises: Educating with Purpose

In this chapter, we'll explore the role of social enterprises in the field of education and how they are driven by a mission to address educational inequities, improve access, and create a positive social impact. Social enterprises bring a unique blend of business acumen and social responsibility to the world of Edu-preneurship.

Defining Social Enterprises in Education

Social enterprises in education are organizations that combine the principles of entrepreneurship with a deep commitment to addressing social issues related to education. They aim to achieve both financial sustainability and meaningful social impact. In the context of education, social enterprises often focus on underserved communities, marginalized groups, and learners who face barriers to access or quality education.

Key Characteristics of Social Enterprises in Education

1. Mission-Driven: The primary goal of social enterprises in education is to create positive social change. Their mission typically revolves around improving access to education, enhancing its quality, or addressing specific educational challenges.

2. Sustainable Business Models: Social enterprises aim to generate revenue to sustain their operations. They often create innovative business models that allow them to fund their social mission while staying financially viable.

3. Partnerships: Collaboration is a cornerstone of social enterprises in education. They often partner with governments, non-profit organizations, schools, and local communities to leverage resources and expertise.

4. Impact Measurement: These organizations place a strong emphasis on measuring and reporting their social impact. They use data to track progress, assess outcomes, and continuously improve their programs.

Examples of Social Enterprises in Education

1. Room to Read: Founded by John Wood, Room to Read is a global organization that focuses on literacy and gender equality in education. It builds libraries, provides books, and offers literacy programs for children in low-income countries.

2. Teach For America: Founded by Wendy Kopp, Teach For America recruits and trains recent college graduates to teach in underserved communities in the United States. Its mission is to close educational gaps and promote educational equity.

3. Barefoot College: Barefoot College, founded by Bunker Roy, empowers rural communities by training local people, often with little or no formal education, to become solar engineers, artisans, and educators. The organization focuses on sustainable development and women's empowerment.

Challenges and Criticisms

Social enterprises in education are not without their challenges and criticisms:

1. Balancing Profit and Impact: Striking a balance between generating revenue and achieving a meaningful social impact can be a complex and ongoing challenge.

2. Measuring Impact: Measuring the true social impact of education can be difficult, as outcomes may not be immediately visible and can take years to manifest.

3. Sustainability: Ensuring long-term financial sustainability while focusing on social impact can be a delicate juggling act for social enterprises.

4. Access and Equity: Even well-intentioned organizations can inadvertently perpetuate certain biases or inequities in their interventions, and addressing these issues requires constant vigilance.

The Future of Social Enterprises in Education

Social enterprises in education are likely to continue playing a vital role in addressing educational inequities and creating positive social impact. As Edu-preneurs explore innovative business models and partnerships, they will contribute to a more equitable and accessible educational landscape. In the chapters ahead, we will explore other Edu-preneurial models and their impact on education, underscoring the diversity and dynamism of this transformative field.

8

Open Educational Resources (OER): Democratizing Learning

In this chapter, we'll explore the role of Open Educational Resources (OER) in education and how they have become a powerful Edupreneurial model for democratizing learning. OER initiatives provide freely accessible educational materials to learners around the world, reducing barriers to education and promoting inclusivity.

Defining Open Educational Resources (OER)

Open Educational Resources (OER) are educational materials, such as textbooks, lesson plans, videos, and interactive simulations, that are made available for free, open access, and use by educators, students, and self-learners. These resources are typically released under licenses that permit users to retain, reuse, revise, remix, and redistribute the content.

Key Characteristics of OER

1. Accessibility: OER materials are accessible to anyone with an internet

connection, breaking down geographical and financial barriers to education.

2. Open Licensing: OER is typically released under open licenses, such as Creative Commons licenses, that allow for various levels of content reuse and adaptation while respecting copyright.

3. Collaboration: OER encourages educators and content creators to collaborate, share knowledge, and continuously improve educational materials.

4. Customization: Educators can customize OER materials to fit the specific needs of their students, making learning more relevant and engaging.

Impact of OER in Education

OER has had a profound impact on education, with several noteworthy outcomes:

1. Cost Savings: OER can significantly reduce the cost of textbooks and course materials for students, making higher education more affordable.

2. Global Reach: OER resources can be accessed by learners worldwide, providing educational opportunities to underserved populations.

3. Pedagogical Innovation: OER encourages innovative teaching methods and empowers educators to tailor materials to their teaching style and students' needs.

4. Collaboration and Knowledge Sharing: The OER community fosters collaboration among educators, researchers, and content creators, enabling the sharing of best practices and resources.

Examples of OER Initiatives

1. MIT OpenCourseWare: The Massachusetts Institute of Technology (MIT) launched MIT OpenCourseWare, providing free access to course materials for virtually all of its undergraduate and graduate-level courses.

2. OpenStax: OpenStax offers free, peer-reviewed, openly licensed textbooks for college and high school courses. These textbooks have been adopted by many institutions to reduce textbook costs for students.

3. Wikimedia Education Program: Wikipedia's Education Program encourages students to contribute to the world's largest open-access encyclopedia as part of their coursework, promoting research and writing skills.

Challenges and Criticisms

OER initiatives face certain challenges and criticisms:

1. Quality Control: Ensuring the quality and accuracy of OER materials can be challenging, as anyone can contribute. Quality control mechanisms are essential to address this concern.

2. Sustainability: Maintaining and updating OER repositories requires financial and institutional support. Sustainability is a significant issue for OER initiatives.

3. Digital Divide: Not all learners have access to the internet or digital devices, limiting their ability to benefit from OER.

4. Copyright and Licensing Issues: Misuse of OER materials or confusion about licensing terms can pose legal and ethical challenges.

The Future of OER and Edu-preneurship

OER has the potential to transform education by making high-quality resources freely available to all. Edu-preneurs, educators, and institutions are likely to continue leveraging the power of OER to create more inclusive and affordable learning experiences. In the chapters ahead, we'll explore additional Edu-preneurial models and their contributions to the ongoing transformation of education.

9

Teacher-Led Innovations: Transforming Education from Within

In this chapter, we'll delve into the Edu-preneurial model of teacher-led innovations, exploring how educators within the traditional educational system are pioneering new teaching methods, curricula, and school programs. These Edu-preneurs work to drive change from within the educational establishment.

The Role of Educators as Edu-preneurs

Educators, who are deeply committed to their students' success, often possess valuable insights into the challenges and opportunities within the traditional education system. Many teachers take on the role of Edu-preneurs, leveraging their expertise and passion to create meaningful change in their classrooms and schools.

Key Characteristics of Teacher-Led Innovations

1. Student-Centered Approaches: Teacher-led innovations often prioritize student needs, engagement, and achievement. They focus on creating

personalized and relevant learning experiences.

2. Innovative Teaching Methods: These initiatives frequently involve the development and implementation of innovative teaching methods and pedagogical approaches that promote critical thinking, problem-solving, and creativity.

3. Curriculum Design and Adaptation: Edu-preneurial educators may redesign curricula to make them more relevant and engaging. They tailor instructional materials to meet the specific needs of their students.

4. Professional Development: Teacher-led innovations can extend to professional development, as educators share best practices and mentor their colleagues.

5. Community Engagement: Many Edu-preneurial teachers actively engage with their local communities to create a more holistic and collaborative educational experience.

Examples of Teacher-Led Innovations

1. Project-Based Learning: Educators often lead initiatives to implement project-based learning (PBL) in their classrooms. PBL emphasizes hands-on, experiential learning and fosters critical thinking and collaboration.

2. Flipped Classrooms: The concept of the flipped classroom, where students engage with instructional content outside of class and use in-class time for discussions and interactive activities, has gained traction thanks to teacher-led innovations.

3. Teacher Professional Learning Communities (PLCs): Educators frequently organize and participate in professional learning communities where they collaborate, share resources, and develop new teaching practices.

Challenges and Criticisms

Teacher-led innovations face certain challenges and criticisms:

1. Resistance to Change: Resistance from other educators, administrators, or institutional policies can hinder the adoption of innovative practices.

2. Resource Limitations: Limited resources, both in terms of time and materials, can constrain the scope and scale of teacher-led initiatives.

3. Assessment and Accountability: Measuring the impact of these innovations can be challenging, particularly within the context of standardized assessments.

The Future of Teacher-Led Innovations and Edu-preneurship

Teacher-led innovations have the potential to be a powerful force for change in education. As educators continue to develop innovative practices, share their successes, and advocate for educational improvement, they will contribute to the ongoing transformation of the educational landscape. In the chapters ahead, we'll explore additional Edu-preneurial models and their role in reshaping education for the better.

10

Edu-preneurship in Policy and Advocacy: Shaping the Future of Education

In this chapter, we will explore the critical role of Edu-preneurship in policy and advocacy, highlighting how Edu-preneurs work to shape the future of education by influencing and driving systemic change through policy initiatives, research, and advocacy efforts.

Edu-preneurship in Policy and Advocacy

Edu-preneurs engaged in policy and advocacy focus on improving education at a systemic level. Their work often extends beyond individual classrooms or schools to impact educational policy, research, and government initiatives.

Key Activities in Edu-preneurship in Policy and Advocacy

1. Research and Data Analysis: Edu-preneurs in this field conduct research to identify educational challenges and opportunities. They collect and analyze data to inform evidence-based policy recommendations.

2. Advocacy and Lobbying: Many Edu-preneurs engage in advocacy efforts,

lobbying for policy changes, funding, and reforms that align with their vision for education.

3. Policy Development: Some Edu-preneurs actively participate in the development of educational policies at the local, state, or national level. They collaborate with policymakers to draft, revise, and implement new regulations and guidelines.

4. Education Campaigns: Edu-preneurs often run public education campaigns to raise awareness about specific educational issues, from early childhood education to college affordability.

5. Community Engagement: These Edu-preneurs may work closely with local communities, parents, and educators to involve them in the policy-making process and garner support for their initiatives.

Examples of Edu-preneurship in Policy and Advocacy

1. Teach Plus: Teach Plus is an organization that empowers teachers to be Edu-preneurs in policy and advocacy. They engage educators in shaping educational policy and driving systemic change by providing them with the tools and opportunities to advocate for student-centered reforms.

2. Education Trust: The Education Trust is a non-profit organization that advocates for educational equity, particularly focusing on closing achievement gaps. They conduct research, develop policy recommendations, and advocate for change at the federal, state, and local levels.

Challenges and Criticisms

Edu-preneurship in policy and advocacy faces certain challenges and criticisms:

1. Political Complexities: The field often involves navigating complex political landscapes, where policy changes may be influenced by various stakeholders and interests.

2. Long Timeframes: Policy changes in education can be slow and take years to implement, making it challenging to see immediate results.

3. Resource Constraints: Advocacy and policy work often require significant financial and human resources, which may limit the influence of smaller organizations or individuals.

The Future of Edu-preneurship in Policy and Advocacy

Edu-preneurs engaged in policy and advocacy will continue to play a crucial role in shaping the future of education. As they advocate for student-centered reforms, equity in education, and data-driven decision-making, they will drive systemic change and work towards creating an education system that serves the diverse needs of all students. In the chapters ahead, we will explore other Edu-preneurial models and their contributions to the ongoing transformation of education.

11

The Global Perspective: Edu-preneurship and International Collaboration

In this chapter, we'll explore the global dimension of Edu-preneurship, focusing on how Edu-preneurs collaborate across borders to address educational challenges and promote international understanding. The exchange of ideas, technologies, and best practices is at the heart of this Edu-preneurial model.

Edu-preneurship on a Global Scale

Education is a global concern, and Edu-preneurs are increasingly looking beyond national borders to create innovative solutions and collaborate on a global scale. International Edu-preneurship focuses on:

1. Cross-Cultural Exchange: Engaging in educational initiatives that foster cross-cultural understanding and collaboration, promoting global citizenship.

2. Adopting Best Practices: Sharing successful educational models, practices, and technologies from one region to another.

3. Addressing Global Challenges: Tackling global educational challenges, such as access to quality education, language barriers, and disparities in educational resources.

Key Activities in International Edu-preneurship

1. Global Partnerships: Edu-preneurs forge partnerships with organizations, governments, and educational institutions in different countries to collaborate on various educational initiatives.

2. Experiential Learning Abroad: They develop programs that provide students with opportunities to learn abroad, engage in cultural exchanges, and gain global perspectives.

3. Multilingual and Multicultural Resources: Edu-preneurs create educational materials that cater to diverse languages and cultural contexts, ensuring that education is accessible and relevant to a global audience.

Examples of International Edu-preneurship

1. e-Learning for Kids: e-Learning for Kids is an organization that provides free, engaging, and fun digital lessons to children worldwide. They focus on making education accessible to children in low-resource settings and offer lessons in multiple languages.

2. Erasmus+ Program: The Erasmus+ Program is a European Union initiative that promotes international collaboration in education. It funds student and staff mobility, partnerships between educational institutions, and innovative projects across various fields.

Challenges and Criticisms

International Edu-preneurship is not without challenges:

1. Cultural Sensitivity: Edu-preneurs must navigate diverse cultural norms, values, and expectations when working in international contexts.

2. Resource Disparities: Educational resource disparities can be significant between countries, making equitable collaboration a challenge.

3. Language Barriers: Language differences can pose communication challenges, requiring efforts to ensure effective knowledge exchange.

The Future of International Edu-preneurship

As the world becomes increasingly interconnected, the role of Edu-preneurship in addressing global educational challenges and fostering international collaboration is likely to grow. Edu-preneurs will continue to develop innovative solutions, share best practices, and work towards a more inclusive and globally-aware education system. In the chapters ahead, we will explore other Edu-preneurial models and their contributions to the transformation of education.

12

Edu-preneurship: Challenges, Ethical Considerations, and the Road Ahead

In this final chapter, we'll reflect on the challenges, ethical considerations, and the future of Edu-preneurship in education. As Edu-preneurs work to transform the educational landscape, they encounter various obstacles and must navigate ethical dilemmas.

Challenges Faced by Edu-preneurs

1. Resistance to Change: Edu-preneurs often encounter resistance from traditional educational systems, which may be resistant to innovation and change.

2. Equity and Access: Ensuring that Edu-preneurial initiatives benefit all students, regardless of their socioeconomic background or location, is a persistent challenge.

3. Resource Limitations: Many Edu-preneurs face resource constraints, whether in terms of funding, time, or human capital.

4. Quality Control: Ensuring the quality of educational innovations, including EdTech tools and materials, is a crucial challenge.

5. Policy and Regulation: Navigating the complex landscape of education policy and regulation can be a daunting task for Edu-preneurs.

Ethical Considerations in Edu-preneurship

1. Privacy and Data Use: Edu-preneurs must consider the privacy of student data and ensure that it is used ethically and responsibly.

2. Equity and Inclusivity: Addressing issues of equity and ensuring that Edu-preneurial initiatives do not exacerbate educational disparities is an ethical imperative.

3. Transparency and Accountability: Edu-preneurs must be transparent about their goals and methodologies and be accountable for the impact of their initiatives.

4. Commercialization of Education: Balancing the commercial interests of Edu-preneurs with the ethical imperative of providing accessible and quality education can be a challenge.

The Road Ahead for Edu-preneurship

The future of Edu-preneurship in education is promising. As Edu-preneurs continue to drive innovation and address educational challenges, several key trends are likely to shape the road ahead:

1. Technological Advancements: The integration of emerging technologies like artificial intelligence, augmented reality, and blockchain will open new avenues for Edu-preneurship in EdTech.

2. Personalized Learning: Personalized learning, driven by data analytics and adaptive technologies, will continue to be a focal point for Edu-preneurs.

3. Global Collaboration: Collaboration between Edu-preneurs from different regions and backgrounds will foster international understanding and bring global perspectives to education.

4. Sustainable Models: Edu-preneurs will focus on sustainable models that balance social impact with financial viability.

5. Advocacy and Policy Impact: Edu-preneurs working in policy and advocacy will continue to influence systemic change and drive student-centered reforms.

Final Thoughts

Edu-preneurship is an evolving field that holds the potential to reshape education for the better. Edu-preneurs, driven by a passion for learning and a commitment to improving educational outcomes, will play a crucial role in creating a more equitable, inclusive, and innovative education system for future generations.

13

Summary

In this comprehensive book on Edu-preneurship, we've explored the transformative role of entrepreneurs in the field of education. The chapters covered various Edu-preneurial models, each contributing to the evolution of education:

- Chapter 1 introduced the concept of Edu-preneurship and its impact on education.

- Chapters 2 through 5 detailed Edu-preneurial models, including the mindset and skillset of Edu-preneurs, historical roots, EdTech innovations, alternative schools, and social enterprises.

- Chapters 6 to 10 delved into specific Edu-preneurial models, such as innovative learning environments, EdTech, open educational resources, teacher-led innovations, and policy and advocacy.

- Chapter 11 highlighted the importance of international collaboration and cross-cultural exchange in Edu-preneurship.

- Chapter 12 addressed the challenges, ethical considerations, and the future of Edu-preneurship, emphasizing the need for ethical practices and social responsibility in educational innovations.

Throughout the book, we've observed how Edu-preneurs are shaping the educational landscape by embracing innovation, technology, and advocacy to provide more equitable, inclusive, and student-centered educational experiences. Edu-preneurship continues to be a dynamic and evolving field with the potential to bring about significant positive changes in education.

www.ingramcontent.com/pod-product-compliance
Lightning Source LLC
LaVergne TN
LVHW012131070526
838202LV00056B/5943